SPACE MYSTERIES

ARE THERE OTHER EARTHS?

Gareth Stevens
Publishing

BY MICHAEL PORTMAN

Please visit our website, www.garethstevens.com. For a free color catalog of all our high-quality books, call toll free 1-800-542-2595 or fax 1-877-542-2596.

Library of Congress Cataloging-in-Publication Data

Portman, Michael, 1976-
 Are there other Earths? / Michael Portman.
      pages ; cm. — (Space mysteries) (What's out there? — The universe in a nutshell — Galaxies and stars —The solar system — The Goldilocks zone — Life in our solar system — Exoplanets — Planet hunting — Hot giants — The transit method — The Kepler space telescope — The search goes on — Into the future.)
 Includes index.
ISBN 978-1-4339-8258-3 (paperback)
ISBN 978-1-4339-8259-0 (6-pack)
ISBN 978-1-4339-8257-6 (library binding)
1. Extrasolar planets—Juvenile literature. 2. Solar system—Juvenile literature. I. Title.
 QB820.P67 2013
 523.2'4—dc23

                                        2012019207

First Edition

Published in 2013 by
Gareth Stevens Publishing
111 East 14th Street, Suite 349
New York, NY 10003

Copyright © 2013 Gareth Stevens Publishing

Designer: Katelyn E. Reynolds
Editor: Therese Shea

Photo credits: Cover, pp. 1, 27 NASA/Ames/JPL-Caltech; cover, pp. 1, 3–32 (background texture) David M. Schrader/Shutterstock.com; pp. 3–32 (fun fact graphic) © iStockphoto.com/spxChrome; p. 5 Photo Researchers/Getty Images; p. 7 Antonio M. Rosario/The Image Bank/Getty Images; p. 9 Artist's Concept/NASA/ESA/STScI; p. 11 martin || fluidworkshop/Shutterstock.com; p. 13 NASA/JPL-Caltech; p. 15 Mark Garlick/Science Photo Library/Getty Images; p. 17 G. Bacon/NASA/ESA/STScI; p. 19 Gregory G. Dimijian/Photo Researchers/Getty Images; p. 21 NASA/ESA/G. Bacon; p. 23 Ian Waldie/Getty Images; p. 25 (both) NASA/Troy Cryder; p. 29 NASA/JPL-Caltech/R. Hunt (SSC-Caltech).

Printed in the United States of America

CPSIA compliance information: Batch #CW13GS: For further information contact Gareth Stevens, New York, New York at 1-800-542-2595.

CONTENTS

Words in the glossary appear in **bold** type the first time they are used in the text.

WHAT'S OUT THERE?

Have you ever looked at the sky on a starry night and wondered what was out there? Are there other planets like Earth? Does life exist on them? If it does, what is it like? For thousands of years, people have been asking these questions.

Since the invention of the **telescope**, we have learned much about the **universe**. However, there's still so much that we don't know. Only recently have we begun to answer the big question: "Are there other Earths?"

OUT OF THIS WORLD!

There are more stars in the sky than grains of sand on all the beaches in the world.

The first planets discovered were Mercury, Venus, Mars, Jupiter, and Saturn. Uranus and Neptune were discovered after the invention of the telescope.

5

OUR UNIVERSE

The universe is big—and it keeps getting bigger. It's so large that we don't even know its exact size. The universe is also old. It's thought to have formed almost 14 billion years ago. Everything that exists is part of the universe.

Astronomers measure the visible parts of the universe using light-years. A light-year is the distance light travels in 1 year. Scientists think it would take light about 93 billion years to cross the visible universe!

OUT OF THIS WORLD!

When we see a star that's 10 light-years away, we're really seeing what that star looked like 10 years ago. It took 10 years for its light to reach Earth!

Light travels nearly 5.9 trillion miles (9.5 trillion km) in 1 year.

7

GALAXIES AND STARS

The universe contains billions of **galaxies** that each have millions or billions of stars. We live in a spiral-shaped galaxy called the Milky Way. The Milky Way is made up of at least 100 billion stars.

A star is a ball of superhot gas. Stars come in many sizes and **temperatures**. Our sun is the star closest to us. Less than 5 percent of the other Milky Way stars are bigger or brighter than our sun. Cooler, smaller stars with a reddish glow are called red dwarfs.

OUT OF THIS WORLD!

The sun is 4.6 billion years old. It's about 333,000 times bigger than Earth. It takes about 8 minutes for sunlight to reach Earth.

The Milky Way galaxy is over 100,000 light-years across.

9

THE SOLAR SYSTEM

A solar system is made up of planets, moons, and anything else that **orbits** a star. There are eight planets in our solar system. The four planets closest to the sun are the small, rocky planets of Mercury, Venus, Earth, and Mars.

The next four planets are Jupiter, Saturn, Uranus, and Neptune. These "gas giants" don't have a solid surface but may have a solid **core**. They're mostly made up of a swirling mix of hydrogen and helium gas.

OUT OF THIS WORLD!

There are 140 known moons in our solar system. Mercury and Venus don't have any moons, while Jupiter has at least 63!

MERCURY

VENUS

EARTH

MARS

JUPITER

SATURN

URANUS

NEPTUNE

Pluto was once considered the ninth planet in our solar system. Its small size and unusual orbit made scientists label it a dwarf planet instead.

PLUTO

11

THE GOLDILOCKS ZONE

Do you remember the fairy tale about Goldilocks and the three bears? In order for a planet to contain life, it has to be in just the right spot in the solar system. Scientists have nicknamed this spot the Goldilocks zone because the planet won't be too hot or too cold there.

The zone is just the right temperature to contain liquid water. Water is necessary to support life as we know it. The Goldilocks zone is also called the habitable zone. "Habitable" means it's fit to be lived in.

OUT OF THIS WORLD!

The temperature of each star decides where its Goldilocks zone is. For cooler stars, the Goldilocks zone is closer to the star. For hotter stars, it's farther away.

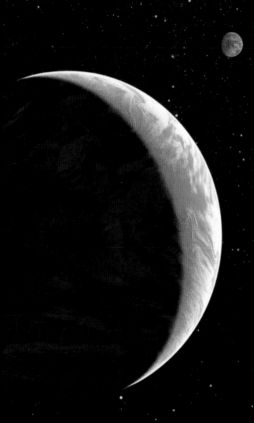

Red dwarfs are cooler than our sun. Therefore, their Goldilocks zone is much closer.

TOO HOT, TOO COLD

The Goldilocks zone in our solar system lies between Venus and Mars. Earth sits comfortably in the middle of the Goldilocks zone. Venus is just a little too close to the sun. That makes it too hot for liquid water. Mars is too far from the sun. Water on Mars' surface is frozen.

Venus and Mars are both very similar to Earth in size. In fact, Venus has often been called Earth's twin. However, neither Venus nor Mars contains life as far as we know.

OUT OF THIS WORLD!

Jupiter and Saturn have moons covered in ice. Some scientists think there may be liquid water below the surface of the ice. Could that water contain life?

Venus

Earth

Mars

Mercury

Earth is the largest of the four planets in our solar system called terrestrial planets. This means they have solid surfaces.

15

EXOPLANETS

For hundreds of years, astronomers suspected there were other planets outside our solar system. They called these planets exoplanets, or extrasolar planets. Unfortunately, they had no way to prove that exoplanets existed. That's because space is too big, stars are too bright, and planets are too dim. Even our strongest telescopes can't see them.

From a long distance, the light from a star outshines any nearby planets. Since exoplanets can't be seen directly, astronomers have come up with other ways of finding them.

OUT OF THIS WORLD!

The brightest star in the sky, besides the sun, is called Sirius. It's about 9 light-years away. As far as we know, there are no planets orbiting Sirius.

Sirius is larger and brighter than our sun. However, it doesn't seem that way to us because it's farther away.

17

PLANET HUNTING

In the 1990s, astronomers discovered the first exoplanets. Astronomers didn't find the exoplanets by spotting them through a telescope, though. Instead, they found them by watching stars.

Planets and stars play a never-ending game of tug-of-war. A star's **gravity** pulls the planet while the planet tries to break free. This is what causes a planet to orbit a star. It also causes the star to "wobble" just the tiniest bit. Astronomers have been able to **detect** this wobble and guess that a planet caused it.

OUT OF THIS WORLD!

Earth's **atmosphere** bends starlight. This is why stars appear to twinkle at night. The atmosphere can also make telescope pictures look blurry.

Computers and special computer programs have made it easier for scientists and stargazers to study the night sky.

19

HOT GIANTS

Within a few years, more and more exoplanets were discovered. Some were labeled "hot Jupiters." These are gas giants about the size of Jupiter that orbit their stars very closely. Life as we know it couldn't exist on planets like these.

The more **mass** the planet has, the more it causes the star to wobble. This movement makes large planets easier to find. Smaller planets cause a smaller wobble. Planets closer to Earth's mass—and more likely to support life as Earth does—are very hard to detect.

OUT OF THIS WORLD!

The first exoplanet discovered orbiting a star was found in 1995. The planet is a hot Jupiter called 51 Pegasi b. It only takes 4 days for 51 Pegasi b to orbit its star.

WASP-12b, left, travels very close to its star. Its orbit makes it the hottest known planet in the Milky Way galaxy.

THE TRANSIT METHOD

Astronomers needed another way to spot smaller exoplanets. They decided to use something called the transit method. When a planet passes in front of a star, it's called a transit event. The light from the star dims very slightly. It's like a moth flying past a lighthouse.

Astronomers can't actually see the planet, but they can measure the amount of light that's blocked. With special tools, astronomers can even detect a small planet.

OUT OF THIS WORLD!

Astronomers measure an exoplanet's orbit. A short orbit means that the planet is close to its star. A longer orbit means that it's farther away.

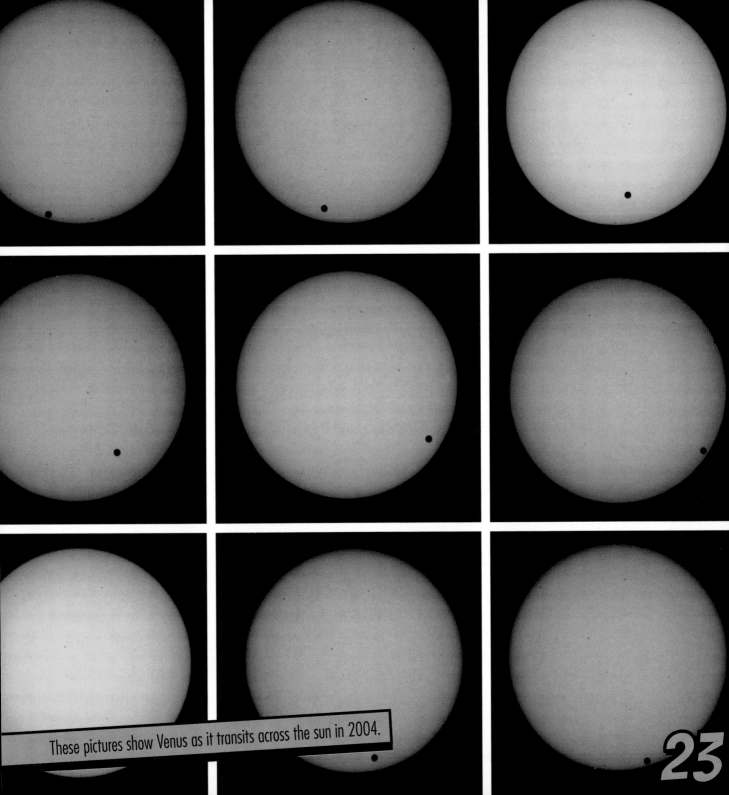

These pictures show Venus as it transits across the sun in 2004.

23

KEPLER

In March 2009, NASA (National Aeronautics and Space Administration) launched the Kepler space telescope. Kepler has one mission: to find Earth-size planets that lie in the Goldilocks zone of their star. Kepler observes over 100,000 stars at once in a small section of space.

The Kepler space telescope uses the transit method to find planets. It observes at least three orbits of a **potential** planet. The first orbit is when the planet is spotted. The second tells astronomers how long the orbit is. A third orbit **confirms** that it's a planet.

OUT OF THIS WORLD!
So far, Kepler has found more than 2,300 potential planets and 61 confirmed planets.

In total, astronomers around the world have discovered over 700 confirmed exoplanets. Kepler, shown here as scientists assemble it, will continue to add to this number.

THE SEARCH GOES ON

Have we found another Earth, a planet that could support human life? So far, the answer is no. Out of the hundreds of planets that have been discovered, only four could potentially hold life.

These four planets, however, appear to have more mass than Earth. This means their gravity is much stronger. It would be impossible or very, very hard just to walk around. Even if these planets have oxygen to breathe, humans would have a tough time living there.

OUT OF THIS WORLD!

The four exoplanets that could potentially hold life are named Gliese 667 Cc, Kepler-22b, HD 85512 b, and Gliese 581d.

Kepler-22 System

Our Solar System

Habitable Zone

Kepler-22b

Mercury

Venus

Earth

Mars

This picture compares Kepler-22b's orbit to Earth's orbit. They're both in Goldilocks zones.

INTO THE FUTURE

Ancient explorers used the stars to help guide them on journeys across the seas. Today, astronomers use the stars to guide them on their journey to find other Earths.

In the 20 years since the first exoplanets were found, many new and exciting discoveries have been made. A true Earth-like planet may already be in the **data** collected by telescopes like Kepler. One day, we might be able to take a clear picture of the surface of an exoplanet. It could be just a matter of time before we discover life!

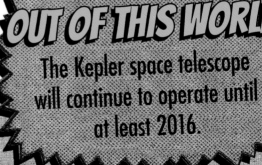

OUT OF THIS WORLD!
The Kepler space telescope will continue to operate until at least 2016.

THE SEARCH FOR HABITABLE EXOPLANETS SO FAR

	total	potential habitable planets
potential exoplanets found by Kepler	2,321	28
potential exoplanets found by other sources	158	1
confirmed exoplanets	763	4

GLOSSARY

astronomer: a person who studies stars, planets, and other heavenly bodies

atmosphere: the mixture of gases that surround a planet

confirm: to find to be true

core: the central part of something

data: facts and figures

detect: to notice or discover the existence of something

galaxy: a large group of stars, planets, gas, and dust that form a unit within the universe

gravity: the force that pulls objects toward the center of a planet or star

mass: the amount of matter in an object

orbit: to travel in a circle or oval around something, or the path used to make that trip

potential: possibly existing

telescope: a tool that makes faraway objects look bigger and closer

temperature: how hot or cold something is

universe: everything that exists

FOR MORE INFORMATION

BOOKS

Kops, Deborah. *Exploring Exoplanets*. Minneapolis, MN: Lerner Classroom Publications, 2012.

Wittenstein, Vicki Oransky. *Planet Hunter: Geoff Marcy and the Search for Other Earths*. Honesdale, PA: Boyds Mills Press, 2010.

WEBSITES

Fun with Astronomy
www.kidsastronomy.com
Play games, watch videos, and learn about space.

Kepler
kepler.nasa.gov
Find out about Kepler's latest discoveries.

NASA Education
www.nasa.gov/audience/forstudents/k-4/index.html
Learn about objects in space and the space program.

INDEX